UK After-Death Checklist - A Complete Guide on What to Do and Who to Notify

UK Edition - 2026

By Wayne Hutchinson & Nadeen Swaby

Published by Handle My Affairs Ltd
United Kingdom

An HMA Support & Wellbeing CIC publication

ISBN: 979-8-89571-327-3

Disclaimer: This publication is intended for informational and educational purposes only. It provides general guidance on the administrative, legal, financial, and practical steps commonly required following a death in the United Kingdom. It does not constitute legal, financial, tax, medical, or professional advice.

While every effort has been made to ensure the information in this guide is accurate and up to date at the time of publication, laws, regulations, eligibility criteria, government services, and contact details may change. The authors and publisher make no representations or warranties as to the ongoing accuracy, completeness, or applicability of the information contained within this book.

Readers are strongly advised to seek independent professional advice from qualified solicitors, probate practitioners, financial advisers, tax specialists, or other appropriate professionals before making decisions or taking action based on the information in this guide.

The authors and publisher accept no responsibility or liability for any loss, damage, or consequences arising directly or indirectly from the use of, or reliance upon, the information contained in this publication.

For enquiries: info@handlemyaffairs.com
For information about bulk purchases, school visits, or workshops, please contact: info@handlemyaffairs.com or visit www.handlemyaffairs.shop

This guide is designed to support and inform during a difficult time, but it should not replace personalised professional advice or emotional support.

Contents

About the Authors

Wayne and Nadeen are committed to supporting individuals and families through grief, loss and end-of-life planning. As a collective, they have undertaken extensive training to strengthen the support they can offer to families. Nadeen has completed Anticipatory Grief Awareness with Cruse Bereavement, while Wayne has completed Bereavement, Grief & Loss training with the National Bereavement Service. In addition to this, between them they have completed a wide range of accredited CPD courses through the Centre of Excellence, including End of Life Therapy, Children and Young People's Mental Health and Wellness, CBT, Life Coaching, Grief and Bereavement Counselling, PTSD Awareness, Journal Therapy, Death Doula training, and SFBT.

Wayne and Nadeen are also both members of the Complementary Medical Association, which supports the professional credibility of their work.

Alongside their formal training, they bring lived experience of personal loss, which deeply shapes their work and the creation of Handle My Affairs — a platform designed to guide families with compassion, clarity and practical support.

All names, organisations, and references within this publication are accurate at the time of publication.

This guide is intended for informational purposes only and does not constitute legal, financial, or professional advice. Readers should consult appropriate professionals for specific advice regarding individual circumstances.

Introduction

Losing a loved one is never easy, and the administrative tasks that follow can feel overwhelming. This guide provides a clear and compassionate roadmap of what to do when someone dies in the UK — including who to notify and how to stay organised throughout the process. It includes legal, financial, and administrative steps, along with key contact details for government bodies, banks, and insurers.

This expanded edition includes critical information that many people don't know about, including the ISA Additional Permitted Subscription (APS), bereavement benefits, Council Tax exemptions, and how to find unclaimed assets. Our goal is to ensure you don't miss out on any financial support or tax reliefs you're entitled to.

Throughout this guide, we highlight time-sensitive actions and common mistakes to avoid. We have included detailed chapters on complex topics like probate, inheritance tax, and intestacy rules, written in plain English to make them accessible to everyone.

Whether you are dealing with a bereavement right now or planning ahead for the future, this guide will be an invaluable resource.

Phase 1: Immediate Steps (First Few Days)

The first steps are focused on legal certainty and immediate practical matters.

Confirm the Death

Contact a GP, NHS 111, or hospital to officially confirm the death.

Obtain Medical Certificate

A doctor will issue a Medical Certificate of Cause of Death (MCCD), unless the death is referred to a Coroner (if sudden, unexpected, or violent). The MCCD is essential for registering the death.

Inform Close Family

Notify next of kin, close family members, and anyone named in the Will. Arrange immediate care for dependents, pets, or vulnerable relatives.

Register the Death

This must be done within 5 days in England and Wales (8 days in Scotland) at the local Register Office where the person died. You will need the MCCD, the deceased's personal details, and their NHS number if known.

Collect Death Certificates

Purchase multiple certified copies of the death certificate (at least 5-10 copies). You will also receive the Certificate for Burial or Cremation. The death certificate is required for all subsequent administrative tasks.

Arrange the Funeral

Check for a Will, funeral plan, or insurance. Choose a funeral director. If the family cannot pay, you may apply for a Funeral Expenses Payment or request a Public Health Funeral through the council.

Phase 2: Notifying Government & Key Agencies

Tell Us Once Service

The most efficient way to notify government departments is through the Tell Us Once service. The registrar will provide a unique reference number to use this free service via GOV.UK.

The Tell Us Once service automatically notifies:

- HM Revenue & Customs (HMRC): Tax, benefits, Self Assessment, National Insurance
- Department for Work and Pensions (DWP): Pensions and benefits
- DVLA: Driving licence
- Passport Office
- Local Council: Council Tax, Blue Badge, housing benefits, electoral roll
- Veterans UK (if applicable)

Key Helplines

- Tell Us Once Helpline: 0800 085 7308
- HMRC Bereavement Helpline: 0300 322 9620
- DWP Bereavement Service: 0800 151 2012
- DVLA: 0300 790 6801

Phase 3: Financial, Legal & Property Matters

Locate the Will

Check the deceased's home, solicitor, bank, or digital vault. Contact the executor named in the Will. If there is no Will, the rules of intestacy apply, and the next of kin must apply for Letters of Administration.

Apply for Probate

Probate (or Confirmation in Scotland) is the legal authority to access and distribute the deceased's bank accounts, property, and investments. It is typically needed if the estate is valued over £5,000 to £15,000, depending on the institution.

Notify Financial Institutions

Contact banks, building societies, pension providers, and investment firms. Use the Death Notification Service to notify multiple banks and building societies (0333 207 6574).

Notify Utility Providers

Contact utility companies (gas, electric, water), phone/broadband, TV licence, and subscriptions. Most utilities have dedicated bereavement teams.

Secure Assets

Lock the property, inform home insurers to ensure cover remains valid, and secure valuables and vehicles. Redirect post for up to 12 months using the Royal Mail Bereavement Service.

Phase 4: Managing the Estate

These tasks are completed by the executor or administrator of the estate after Probate is granted.

Value the Estate

Determine the value of all assets and liabilities, including property, bank accounts, investments, personal possessions, and any debts.

Pay Inheritance Tax

If Inheritance Tax (IHT) is due, it must be paid to HMRC. You may need to pay at least some of the tax before you can obtain the Grant of Probate.

Pay Debts and Liabilities

All outstanding debts must be settled before distributing the estate. This includes mortgages, loans, credit cards, utility bills, and funeral expenses.

Distribute Assets

The remaining assets are distributed to the beneficiaries according to the Will or intestacy rules. Prepare detailed estate accounts for the beneficiaries to approve before making final payments.

Phase 5: Digital Legacy and Online Accounts

Dealing with digital accounts is a crucial modern task. You will need to decide whether to memorialise (keep the account as a tribute) or delete the account.

Facebook

Memorialisation (Legacy Contact can manage) or Deletion. Requires proof of death.

Instagram

Memorialisation or Deletion. Requires proof of death.

Google

Inactive Account Manager (if set up) or legal documentation required.

Apple

Digital Legacy (if set up). Allows a designated Legacy Contact to access data.

X (formerly Twitter)

Deactivation only (no memorialisation option).

Chapter 1: A Guide to UK Bereavement Benefits

Losing a partner is a devastating experience, and the financial impact can add significant stress during an already difficult time. The UK government provides financial support to help ease this burden through a system of bereavement benefits. This chapter explains the main benefit available, the Bereavement Support Payment (BSP), as well as older benefits you might still be receiving.

Understanding Bereavement Support Payment (BSP)

Bereavement Support Payment is the primary benefit for those whose spouse, civil partner, or cohabiting partner died on or after 6 April 2017. It is designed to provide a financial cushion during the initial period of bereavement and is not means-tested, meaning your income or savings will not affect your eligibility.

Who is Eligible for BSP?

To be eligible for Bereavement Support Payment, you must meet several criteria at the time of your partner's death:

- You must have been under the State Pension age.

- You must have been living in the UK or a country that pays bereavement benefits.

- You must have been married to, in a civil partnership with, or living with your partner as if you were married.

In addition, your late partner must have either:

- Paid a certain amount of Class 1 or Class 2 National Insurance contributions in any single tax year since 1975.

- Died as a result of an accident at work or a disease caused by work.

***Important Note:** Even if you are unsure whether your partner paid enough National Insurance, you should still make a claim. The Bereavement Service will check the contribution record for you.*

How Much Will You Receive?

The amount of BSP you receive depends on your circumstances, specifically whether you were responsible for a child at the time of your partner's death.

Higher Rate Eligibility: You qualify for the higher rate if, at the time of your partner's death, you were pregnant or entitled to Child Benefit. This now includes cohabiting partners with dependent children, following a landmark law change.

The Critical Importance of Claiming on Time

BSP is paid for a maximum of 18 months, and the window to claim is time-sensitive. To receive the full amount, you must claim within 3 months of your partner's death.

- **Claim within 3 months**: You receive the lump-sum first payment and all 18 monthly instalments.

- **Claim between 3 and 12 months**: You will receive the lump-sum payment, but you will get fewer monthly instalments.

- **Claim between 12 and 21 months**: You will not receive the lump-sum payment, but you can still get some of the monthly instalments.

- **Claim after 21 months**: You will usually not be able to get any payment.

***Action Point:** Make claiming BSP a priority. The deadline is strict, and missing it can result in losing thousands of pounds in support.*

How to Claim BSP

You can claim Bereavement Support Payment in one of three ways:

1. **Online**: Via the GOV.UK website, which is the quickest

    method.

2. **By Phone**: Call the DWP Bereavement Service at 0800 151

    2012.

3. **By Post**: Download a BSP1 form from the GOV.UK

    website.

How BSP Affects Other Benefits

For the first year, BSP payments are not counted as income for means-tested benefits like Universal Credit. This means your other benefits will not be affected during this period. However, after one year, any remaining money from your lump-sum payment may be counted as savings, which could impact your eligibility for other benefits.

Older Bereavement Benefits

If your partner died before 6 April 2017, you might be receiving one of the older bereavement benefits. These are no longer open to new claims but will continue to be paid if you are still eligible.

- **Widowed Parent's Allowance**: Paid to widowed parents with dependent children. Payments continue as long as you receive Child Benefit.

- **Bereavement Allowance**: Paid for 52 weeks to widows, widowers, or surviving civil partners who were aged 45 or over at the time of their partner's death.

If you are receiving these benefits, your payments will continue as normal. You do not need to do anything.

This chapter provides a general overview. For detailed information and to make a claim, please visit the official GOV.UK website.

Chapter 2: The Inheritance You Didn't Know You Had: ISA Additional Permitted Subscription (APS)

When a spouse or civil partner passes away, their Individual Savings Account (ISA) doesn't have to lose its tax-free status. A little-known but incredibly valuable rule allows the surviving partner to inherit a special ISA allowance, known as the Additional Permitted Subscription (APS). This is one of the most frequently missed opportunities in after-death financial administration, and understanding it could save you a significant amount in tax.

This chapter demystifies the ISA APS, explaining what it is, who qualifies, and how to claim it.

What is an Additional Permitted Subscription (APS)?

An APS is a one-off, additional ISA allowance available to the surviving spouse or civil partner of a deceased ISA holder. It is equal to the value of the deceased's ISA at the time of their death. This allowance is in addition to your own annual ISA allowance (£20,000 for the 2025/26 tax year). This means you can shelter a much larger sum of money from tax in the year following your partner's death.

> **Key Takeaway:** *The APS is not the money from the ISA itself, but an extra allowance to put more money into your own ISA, tax-free. You are eligible for this allowance even if you do not inherit the actual cash or investments from your partner's ISA.*

Who is Eligible for the APS Allowance?

The eligibility criteria are straightforward:

- You must be the surviving spouse or civil partner of the
  deceased.

- You and your partner must have been living together at the
  time of their death (not separated by a court order, deed of
  separation, or in circumstances where the marriage had
  broken down).

That's it. Unmarried partners are not eligible for the APS
allowance.

How Much is the APS Allowance?

For deaths on or after 6 April 2018, the rules are generous. The APS allowance is the higher of two values:

1. The value of the deceased's ISA(s) at the date of their death.

2. The value of the deceased's ISA(s) at the date the account is closed (which can be up to 3 years after death).

This protects the surviving spouse from any fall in the value of the investments after the date of death and allows them to benefit from any growth.

In Scenario A, the surviving spouse can subscribe up to £55,000 into their own ISA, in addition to their personal £20,000 allowance for that year, for a total of £75,000.

The Critical Time Limits for Using Your APS

Like many financial benefits, the APS allowance has a deadline. You must use the allowance within a specific timeframe, or you will lose it.

- **For cash subscriptions**: You have three years from the date of death to use the allowance.

- **For 'in specie' subscriptions (transferring the actual investments):** You have 180 days from the date the investments are distributed to you from the estate.

Given these generous timeframes, there is no need to rush, but it is crucial to be aware of the final deadline.

How to Claim and Use Your APS Allowance

The process involves contacting an ISA provider. You have two main options:

1. **Use the deceased's ISA provider:** You can make your

   APS with the provider who held your late partner's ISA.

2. **Use your own or a different provider**: You can transfer

   the APS allowance to another ISA manager of your choice.

   Not all providers accept APS transfers, so you must check

   with them first.

To make the claim, you will typically need to complete a form and provide:

- Your personal details.

- The deceased's details (name, address, date of death,

  National Insurance number).

- A copy of the death certificate.

- A copy of your marriage or civil partnership certificate.

Cash vs. 'In Specie' Subscriptions

You can use your APS allowance in two ways:

- **Cash Subscription**: You can fund the subscription with cash. This can be from the inherited ISA, or from any other money you have.

- **'In Specie' Subscription**: If you inherit the actual investments (shares, funds, etc.) from your partner's ISA, you can transfer them directly into your own ISA without selling them first. This can only be done with the deceased's original ISA provider.

> **Action Point:** If you have inherited an ISA, contact the ISA provider and ask about their process for using your Additional Permitted Subscription. Do not simply cash in the ISA without exploring this option, or you could miss out on a valuable tax benefit.

This information is based on current UK tax law, which can change. Always confirm the latest rules with your ISA provider or a financial advisor.

Chapter 3: Navigating the Probate Process

After a person dies, their assets, money, and property—
collectively known as their estate—must be legally dealt with.
The official process of managing this estate is called probate.
For many, the term is shrouded in mystery and can seem
intimidating. This chapter provides a clear, step-by-step guide
to understanding what probate is, when it is needed, and how to
navigate the process.

What is Probate?

Probate is the legal and financial process of dealing with a
deceased person's estate. It involves identifying all assets and
liabilities, paying any taxes and debts, and distributing the
remaining assets to the rightful beneficiaries. The process is
overseen by the High Court and gives the executor (or
administrator) the legal authority to act on behalf of the estate.

This authority is granted in a document called a Grant of
Representation. There are two main types:

1. **Grant of Probate:** This is issued to the executor(s) named

   in the deceased's will.

2. **Grant of Letters of Administration:** This is issued to the

   next of kin (known as the administrator) when the deceased

   has died without a will (this is known as dying 'intestate').

When is Probate Required?

Probate is not always necessary. It generally depends on the value and complexity of the estate. Many banks and financial institutions will release funds without a Grant of Probate if the amount held is small. This is often referred to as the 'small estates' process.

> **Rule of Thumb:** *If the estate includes property, or if the total value of the assets is over £15,000, you will likely need to apply for probate.*

The Probate Process: A Step-by-Step Guide

The probate process can be broken down into several key stages. While the timeline can vary depending on the complexity of the estate, the steps are broadly the same.

Step 1: Value the Estate (2-4 weeks)

The first task is to identify and value all the assets and liabilities of the deceased as at the date of their death. This includes:

- **Assets**: Property, bank accounts, savings, investments, shares, premium bonds, cars, jewellery, and other personal possessions.

- **Liabilities**: Mortgages, loans, credit card debts, utility bills, and funeral expenses.

You will need to write to all relevant institutions to get precise valuations.

Step 2: Complete the Inheritance Tax (IHT) Return (2-4 weeks)

Before you can apply for probate, you must complete an Inheritance Tax return for HMRC.

- **If no IHT is due**: You will complete a shorter form (IHT205).

- **If IHT is due**: You must complete the full IHT400 form and pay at least some of the tax due. You cannot get the Grant of Probate until HMRC has processed the IHT return and issued a unique code.

Step 3: Apply for the Grant of Representation (2-8 weeks)

Once the IHT forms are submitted, you can apply for the Grant of Probate (or Letters of Administration). This can be done online or by post. You will need to provide the original will (if there is one) and the death certificate.

The current fee for applying for probate is £273 for estates over £5,000 (as of 2026). There is no fee for estates under £5,000.

Step 4: Administer the Estate (4-12 weeks)

Once the Grant of Representation is received, you are legally authorised to administer the estate. This involves:

1. Closing bank accounts and collecting all funds.

2. Selling or transferring assets such as property and shares.

3. Paying all debts and liabilities, including any outstanding

IHT.

Step 5: Distribute the Assets (1-2 weeks)

The final step is to distribute the remaining assets to the beneficiaries according to the will or the rules of intestacy. It is crucial to prepare detailed estate accounts showing all money in and out of the estate and have them approved by the main beneficiaries before making the final payments.

How Long Does Probate Take?

For a straightforward estate, the entire process can take between 6 to 12 months. However, complex estates, especially those involving foreign assets, business interests, or disputes, can take significantly longer.

> **Action Point:** Keep meticulous records of all communications, valuations, and transactions. This will be essential for preparing the estate accounts and answering any queries from beneficiaries.

The probate process can be complex. If you are unsure about any aspect, it is always advisable to seek professional legal advice.

Chapter 4: Understanding Inheritance Tax (IHT)

Inheritance Tax (IHT) is often misunderstood and can be a source of considerable anxiety. It is a tax on the estate (the property, money, and possessions) of someone who has died. However, with careful planning and knowledge of the available allowances, many estates will not have to pay any IHT at all. This chapter breaks down the key components of IHT, including thresholds, allowances, and important reliefs.

The Basics of Inheritance Tax

As of the 2025/26 tax year, the standard rate of Inheritance Tax is 40%. This is only charged on the part of the estate that is above a certain threshold. For most people, there are two main allowances that can be used to reduce or eliminate an IHT bill.

1. The Nil-Rate Band (NRB)

Every individual has a Nil-Rate Band (NRB), which is a threshold below which no IHT is paid.

- **Current NRB**: £325,000

This means that if the total value of the estate is less than £325,000, there is generally no IHT to pay.

2. The Residence Nil-Rate Band (RNRB)

In addition to the NRB, there is an extra allowance if you pass on your main home to your direct descendants. This is known as the Residence Nil-Rate Band (RNRB).

- **Current RNRB**: £175,000

Direct descendants include children, grandchildren, and stepchildren. To qualify, the deceased must have owned the property and lived in it at some point.

By combining these two allowances, an individual can potentially pass on up to £500,000 tax-free (£325,000 NRB + £175,000 RNRB).

The Power of Transferable Allowances

One of the most significant aspects of IHT planning is that any unused allowances can be transferred to a surviving spouse or civil partner. This means that a married couple or civil partners can combine their allowances.

This doubling-up of allowances means that a married couple can potentially leave an estate of up to £1 million to their direct descendants without paying any Inheritance Tax.

> **Example:** John dies and leaves his entire estate of £400,000 to his wife, Mary. This transfer is completely tax-free (see Spouse Exemption below). When Mary later dies, her estate can use her own £500,000 allowance plus John's unused £500,000 allowance, allowing her to pass on up to £1 million tax-free to their children.

Key IHT Exemptions and Reliefs

Beyond the main allowances, there are several other important exemptions and reliefs that can reduce an IHT bill.

Spouse or Civil Partner Exemption

Any assets left to a surviving spouse or civil partner are completely exempt from IHT, provided the surviving partner is domiciled in the UK. This is an unlimited exemption and is one of the cornerstones of IHT planning for couples.

Charity Exemption

Any gifts left to a qualifying UK charity in a will are exempt from IHT. Furthermore, if at least 10% of the net estate is left to charity, the IHT rate on the rest of the estate is reduced from 40% to 36%.

Business and Agricultural Relief

- **Business Relief**: This can reduce the value of a business or its assets by up to 100% for IHT purposes. This is a vital relief for business owners to ensure their business can continue after their death.

- **Agricultural Relief**: This can reduce the value of agricultural land and property by up to 100%. This is designed to help keep farms within the family.

Annual Gift Exemption

During their lifetime, an individual can give away up to £3,000 each tax year without it being added to the value of their estate. This is known as the annual exemption. If you don't use it one year, you can carry it forward to the next, but for one year only.

Paying the Inheritance Tax Bill

If there is an IHT liability, it must be paid to HMRC by the end of the sixth month after the person's death. If it is not paid on time, HMRC will charge interest.

The tax on assets like cash and investments must be paid before probate is granted. However, the tax on property can be paid in annual instalments over 10 years, although interest will be charged.

> ***Action Point:** Valuing the estate and calculating IHT can be complex. It is one of the key responsibilities of the executor. If the estate is likely to be subject to IHT, it is highly recommended to seek professional advice from a solicitor or tax advisor.*

This chapter provides a summary of the main IHT rules. The regulations are complex and subject to change. For official guidance, refer to the GOV.UK website.

Chapter 5: What Happens When There is No Will? The Rules of Intestacy

A will is a vital legal document that sets out a person's wishes for how their estate should be distributed after they die. However, a surprising number of people die without a valid will in place. When this happens, the law has to step in to decide who inherits the estate. This is known as dying intestate, and the distribution of assets is governed by a strict set of legal principles called the Rules of Intestacy.

This chapter explains how these rules work and highlights some of the common pitfalls and misconceptions.

The Hierarchy of Inheritance

The Rules of Intestacy follow a rigid hierarchy, with the surviving spouse or civil partner having the primary claim, followed by children, and then other relatives in a specific order. It is crucial to understand that unmarried partners and cohabiting couples have no automatic right to inherit under these rules.

Scenario 1: Surviving Spouse/Civil Partner and Children

This is the most common scenario, and the rules depend on the value of the estate. As of 2025, the statutory legacy (the fixed sum the spouse receives) is £322,000.

- **If the estate is worth up to £322,000**: The surviving

  spouse or civil partner inherits the entire estate.

- **If the estate is worth over £322,000**: The surviving spouse

  or civil partner receives:

  All the deceased's personal possessions.

  The first £322,000 of the estate.

  Half of the remaining balance of the estate.

- The children inherit the other half of the remaining balance,

  split equally between them.

***Example:** David dies intestate, leaving an estate worth £522,000. He is survived by his wife, Sarah, and their two children. Under the rules: 1. Sarah receives the first £322,000. 2. The remaining balance is £200,000 (£522,000 - £322,000). 3. Sarah receives half of this (£100,000). 4. The two children share the other half, receiving £50,000 each. In total, Sarah inherits £422,000, and each child inherits £50,000.*

Scenario 2: Surviving Spouse/Civil Partner but No Children

If there is a surviving spouse or civil partner but no children, the situation is simple: the surviving spouse or civil partner inherits the entire estate.

Scenario 3: No Surviving Spouse/Civil Partner

If there is no surviving spouse or civil partner, the estate is distributed to other relatives in a strict order of priority:

1. **Children**: The entire estate is shared equally among the children. If a child has already died, their share passes to their own children (the deceased's grandchildren).

2. **Parents**: If there are no children, the estate passes to the deceased's parents in equal shares.

3. **Full Siblings**: If there are no surviving parents, the estate is shared among the deceased's full-blood brothers and sisters.

4. **Half Siblings**: If there are no full siblings, the estate is shared among half-brothers and half-sisters.

5. **Grandparents**: If there are no siblings, the estate passes to the grandparents.

6. **Full Aunts and Uncles**: If there are no grandparents, the estate is shared among full-blood aunts and uncles.

7. **Half Aunts and Uncles**: If there are no full aunts and uncles, the estate is shared among half-blood aunts and uncles.

What if There Are No Surviving Relatives?

If a person dies intestate and has no surviving relatives who can inherit under the rules, their estate passes to the Crown. This is known as Bona Vacantia (Latin for 'vacant goods').

The Plight of Unmarried Partners

One of the most critical takeaways from the Rules of Intestacy is the lack of provision for unmarried or cohabiting partners. No matter how long a couple has been together, the surviving partner has no automatic right to inherit if there is no will. This can lead to devastating consequences, where a long-term partner can be left with nothing, while the estate passes to distant relatives.

In such cases, the only option for the surviving partner is to make a legal claim against the estate for financial provision under the Inheritance (Provision for Family and Dependants) Act 1975. This can be a complex, costly, and emotionally draining process, with no guarantee of success.

> **Action Point:** *The only way to ensure your partner is provided for after your death is to make a will. The Rules of Intestacy offer no protection for unmarried couples.*

This chapter provides a general guide. The Rules of Intestacy are complex, and you should seek legal advice if you are dealing with an intestate estate.

Chapter 6: Joint Accounts and Property: What Happens After Death?

Many couples and families in the UK own assets jointly, such as bank accounts and property. This is often done for convenience, but the way these assets are owned has significant legal implications after one of the owners dies. The key principle to understand is the Right of Survivorship.

This chapter explains how jointly owned assets are treated after death and clarifies the important distinction between owning property as 'joint tenants' versus 'tenants in common'.

Joint Bank and Savings Accounts

Most joint bank or savings accounts in the UK are held on a 'joint beneficial interest' basis. This means that both account holders have an equal right to the money in the account. When one of the account holders dies, the Right of Survivorship automatically applies.

- What is the Right of Survivorship? This legal principle means that the deceased person's share of the account automatically passes to the surviving account holder(s). The money does not form part of the deceased's estate and is not covered by their will or the rules of intestacy.

This process is usually straightforward. The surviving account holder will need to take a copy of the death certificate to the bank. The bank will then typically:

1. Remove the deceased's name from the account.

2. Transfer the account into the sole name of the survivor.

> ***Important Note:** While the money in a joint account passes directly to the survivor, for Inheritance Tax (IHT) purposes, HMRC will still consider the deceased's share of the money (usually 50%) as part of their estate. This must be declared when valuing the estate.*

Jointly Owned Property: A Tale of Two Tenancies

When it comes to property, the situation is more complex. There are two ways a property can be jointly owned in England and Wales, and they have very different consequences upon death.

1. Joint Tenants

This is the most common way for married couples and civil partners to own their home. As with joint bank accounts, the Right of Survivorship applies.

- **How it works**: Both owners own 100% of the property together. There are no separate shares. When one joint tenant dies, their ownership automatically passes to the surviving joint tenant(s).

- **Impact on the Will**: The property does not pass under the terms of the deceased's will. The transfer to the survivor is automatic and overrides any wishes stated in the will.

- **Probate**: Probate is not usually required to transfer the property to the surviving owner. The survivor simply needs to update the property records at HM Land Registry using form DJP (Deceased Joint Proprietor).

2. Tenants in Common

This method of ownership is more common for unmarried partners, friends, or family members buying property together. It is also used by couples who want to have more control over who inherits their share of the property.

- **How it works**: Each owner holds a distinct, separate share of the property. This can be 50/50, or any other proportion (e.g., 60/40, 70/30).

- **No Right of Survivorship**: When a tenant in common dies, their share of the property does not automatically pass to the other owner. Instead, it forms part of their estate and is passed on according to their will or the rules of intestacy.

- **Impact on the Will**: The deceased's share of the property is a key part of their estate and must be distributed as per their will. This allows a tenant in common to leave their share to their children, another relative, or anyone they choose.

- **Probate**: A Grant of Probate will be required to deal with the deceased's share of the property.

How to Check Your Ownership Status

You can find out how you own your property by checking the title deeds or by obtaining a copy of the title register from HM Land Registry. If the register states, "No disposition by a sole proprietor of the registered estate (except a trust corporation) under which capital money arises is to be registered unless authorised by an order of the court," this usually indicates you are tenants in common.

> **Action Point:** Understanding how you own your property is a critical part of estate planning. If you are tenants in common, it is essential that you have a valid will in place to determine who will inherit your share.

This chapter provides a general overview. Property law is complex, and you should always seek legal advice when dealing with property transfers after a death.

Chapter 7: Council Tax After a Death: Exemptions and Discounts You Need to Know About

When a person dies, their Council Tax liability does not simply disappear. However, there are important exemptions and discounts available that can save the estate—and the bereaved—a significant amount of money. Many people are unaware of these reliefs and end up paying Council Tax when they don't have to. This chapter outlines the key rules you need to be aware of.

The Single Person Discount: An Immediate 25% Reduction

If the deceased lived with one other adult, the surviving person is now the sole adult occupant of the property. As a result, they are entitled to a Single Person Discount on their Council Tax bill.

- **Discount Amount**: 25% off the total bill.

- **How to Apply**: You must apply for this discount through the local council. It is not applied automatically. You will usually need to provide a copy of the death certificate.

  Action Point: *If you are now living alone, contact your local council immediately to apply for the Single Person Discount. This can save you hundreds of pounds a year.*

The Empty Property Exemption (Class F Exemption)

If the deceased lived alone, their property will become empty upon their death. In this situation, the property may be exempt from Council Tax altogether. This is known as a Class F Exemption.

This exemption is designed to give the executor or administrator time to deal with the estate without the pressure of ongoing Council Tax bills. The exemption is split into two parts.

Part 1: The Pre-Probate Exemption

From the date of death until the Grant of Probate (or Letters of Administration) is issued, an empty property is fully exempt from Council Tax.

- **Duration**: This exemption lasts for as long as it takes to get the Grant of Representation. There is no time limit on this part of the exemption.

- **Condition**: The property must remain unoccupied.

Part 2: The Post-Probate Exemption

Once probate has been granted, the property can remain exempt for a further period of up to six months.

- **Duration**: A maximum of six months from the date the Grant of Representation is issued.

- **Conditions**: The exemption will end if the property is sold, transferred to a beneficiary, or becomes occupied.

In total, an empty property can be exempt from Council Tax for the entire probate period plus an additional six months. This can represent a saving of thousands of pounds for the estate.

What Happens When the Exemption Ends?

If the property remains empty and unsold after the exemption period has finished, the full Council Tax charge will become due. The liability for this falls to the estate, and the bill must be paid by the executor or administrator. Some councils may even charge a premium for long-term empty properties.

How to Inform the Council of a Death

It is the responsibility of the executor or administrator to inform the local council of the death. You will need to provide:

- The name of the deceased person.

- The address of the property.

- The date of death.

- The name and address of the executor or administrator.

- A copy of the death certificate.

It is important to keep the council updated on the progress of the estate administration, particularly when probate is granted and when the property is sold or transferred.

***Action Point:** Do not assume the council will know about the death. Contact them as soon as possible to ensure any discounts or exemptions are applied correctly and to avoid any unnecessary bills being sent to the property.*

Council Tax rules are set by local authorities, and there can be minor variations. Always check the specific rules with the relevant council.

Chapter 8: Dealing with Premium Bonds and other NS&I Products

National Savings & Investments (NS&I) is a state-owned savings bank in the UK, and one of the largest savings organisations in the country. Many people who die will have money held in NS&I products, with Premium Bonds being by far the most popular. As an executor or administrator, it is your responsibility to deal with these assets as part of the estate.

This chapter explains what happens to Premium Bonds after death and how to claim the funds from all NS&I products.

Premium Bonds: A Special Case

Premium Bonds are a unique savings product where the interest is paid out via a monthly prize draw, with prizes ranging from £25 to £1 million. A common question is what happens to these bonds when the holder dies.

Do They Still Win Prizes?

Yes. After the holder has died, their Premium Bonds can remain in the prize draw for up to 12 months from the date of death.

*   **How it works**: Any prizes won during this 12-month period

    are paid by cheque to the person who has been nominated

    to administer the estate.

- **What to do**: There is no need to do anything immediately. The bonds will be automatically entered into the draws. You can choose to cash them in at any time during this period, but once cashed in, they will no longer be eligible for prizes.

After 12 months, the bonds are automatically cashed in, and the money is held by NS&I until the executor or administrator makes a claim.

***Action Point:** Before rushing to cash in Premium Bonds, consider leaving them in the monthly prize draws for the full 12 months. There is a chance the estate could benefit from a tax-free prize.*

How to Claim Funds from NS&I

The process for claiming money from any NS&I product—be it Premium Bonds, Savings Certificates, Income Bonds, or a Direct Saver account—is the same. The claim is made through the NS&I bereavement service.

The Claims Process

1. **Complete the Bereavement Claim Form**: This can be done online on the NS&I website, which is the quickest and easiest method. Alternatively, you can download a paper form or call NS&I to request one.

2. **Provide Necessary Documents**: You will need to provide some key documents along with your claim form:

    *   A copy of the death certificate.
    *   A copy of the will (if there is one).
    *   The Grant of Probate or Letters of Administration (if required).

When is Probate Required for NS&I?

NS&I has its own rules about when they require a Grant of Representation. They will often release funds without probate if the total amount held with them is below a certain threshold.

- Check the Threshold: This threshold can change, so it is important to check the current limit on the NS&I website. If the total value of all NS&I holdings is below this limit, you may be able to close the accounts without needing to go through the full probate process.

  ***Finding Unknown NS&I Holdings:** If you are unsure whether the deceased had any NS&I products, you can use the NS&I tracing service. There is also a service called My Lost Account which can help trace lost bank accounts and NS&I products.*

How to Contact NS&I

- **Website**: The NS&I website (nsandi.com) has a dedicated bereavement section with all the necessary forms and guidance.

- **Phone**: You can call their customer service team for free on 08085 007 007.

What About Junior ISAs and Child Trust Funds?

If the deceased was the registered contact for a Junior ISA or Child Trust Fund held with NS&I, the new guardian or the person with parental responsibility for the child will need to become the new registered contact. This involves completing a change of registered contact form and providing the child's birth certificate and the death certificate of the former registered contact.

Dealing with NS&I is usually a straightforward part of administering an estate. Their dedicated bereavement team is there to help guide you through the process.

Chapter 9: Making a Life Insurance Claim

A life insurance policy is a contract with an insurer that promises to pay out a sum of money upon the death of the insured person. For many families, a life insurance payout is a vital financial lifeline, providing security at a time of great uncertainty. However, the process of making a claim can seem daunting.

This chapter explains the different types of life insurance, how to make a claim, and the critical importance of writing a policy 'in trust'.

Types of Life Insurance

There are several different types of life insurance policies, but they all serve the same fundamental purpose: to provide a financial payout upon death.

- **Term Life Insurance**: This is the most common type. It covers the policyholder for a fixed period (the 'term'), for example, 25 years. If the person dies within the term, the policy pays out. If they survive the term, the policy ends, and there is no payout.

- **Whole-of-Life Insurance**: This type of policy covers the person for their entire life, so it is guaranteed to pay out eventually, provided the premiums have been kept up.

- **Mortgage Protection Insurance**: This is a specific type of term insurance designed to pay off the policyholder's mortgage if they die.

- **Critical Illness Cover**: While not strictly life insurance, these policies are often sold alongside them. They pay out a lump sum if the policyholder is diagnosed with a serious illness, and some may include a death benefit.

The Crucial Difference: Policies In Trust vs. Not In Trust

How a life insurance policy is set up determines how the payout is handled after death. This is one of the most important distinctions in all of estate planning.

Policies Written 'In Trust'

When a life insurance policy is 'written in trust', it means that the policy is legally separated from the deceased's estate. The policy is held by trustees for the benefit of named beneficiaries.

- **Direct Payout**: The insurance payout goes directly to the beneficiaries. It does not go into the estate.

- **No Probate Needed**: Because the money is not part of the estate, the beneficiaries do not have to wait for a Grant of Probate to receive the funds. This makes the process much faster.

- **No Inheritance Tax**: The payout is not subject to Inheritance Tax. This can result in a huge tax saving.

Policies Not Written In Trust

If a policy is not written in trust, the payout is made to the deceased's legal estate.

- **Forms Part of the Estate**: The money is added to the overall value of the estate.

- **Probate Required**: The funds cannot be released until a Grant of Probate has been issued, which can take many months.

- **Subject to Inheritance Tax**: The payout increases the value of the estate and could therefore be subject to 40% Inheritance Tax.

***Action Point:** Writing a life insurance policy in trust is one of the simplest and most effective estate planning tools available. It is usually free to do when you take out the policy. If you have life insurance, check if it is written in trust.*

How to Make a Life Insurance Claim

If you are the beneficiary or the executor of an estate, you will need to contact the insurance company to start the claims process.

1. **Find the Policy Documents**: The first step is to locate the life insurance policy documents. These will contain the policy number and the contact details for the insurer.

2. **Contact the Insurer**: Notify the insurer's bereavement or claims department of the death. They will guide you through their specific process.

3. **Complete the Claim Form**: The insurer will provide you with a claim form to complete.

4. **Provide Necessary Documents**: You will typically need to provide:

    * The original policy document (if available).
    * A certified copy of the death certificate.
    * Proof of your identity.
    * The Grant of Probate (if the policy was not in trust).

What if You Can't Find the Policy?

If you believe the deceased had a life insurance policy but you cannot find the documents, you should not give up. You can try:

- Checking bank statements for payments to an insurance company.

- Contacting the deceased's employer, as they may have had a 'death in service' policy.

- Using a tracing service, such as the Unclaimed Assets Register, although this may involve a fee.

Life insurance payouts can provide essential financial support to a grieving family. Understanding how the policy is set up is key to ensuring a smooth and tax-efficient claims process.

Chapter 10: The Hunt for Hidden Treasure: Finding Unclaimed Assets and Lost Accounts

It is estimated that there are billions of pounds lying dormant in the UK in forgotten bank accounts, pensions, and investments. When a person dies, it is the executor's duty to track down all of their assets, and this includes searching for any that may have been lost or forgotten over the years.

Failing to conduct a thorough search can mean that beneficiaries miss out on a significant inheritance. This chapter provides a guide to the free services available to help you trace these hidden financial treasures.

The Scale of the Problem

People lose track of accounts for many reasons. They may have moved house and forgotten to update their address, changed jobs and lost touch with a pension provider, or simply opened an account many years ago and forgotten about it. Over time, these accounts become 'dormant'.

The good news is that this money is not lost forever. It is protected and can be reclaimed by the original owner or by the executor of their estate.

How to Search for Lost and Dormant Accounts

There are several free and official services designed to help you trace lost assets. You should be wary of any company that charges a large fee for this service, as you can do it yourself for free.

1. For Lost Bank and Savings Accounts: My Lost Account

My Lost Account is a free online service that can help you trace lost bank accounts, building society accounts, and National Savings & Investments (NS&I) products.

- **How it works**: The service is a joint venture by UK Finance, the Building Societies Association, and NS&I. You complete a single online form, and the service will search the records of all participating banks and building societies.

- **What you need**: You will need to provide the deceased's personal details, including their name, date of birth, and previous addresses.

- **Website**: mylostaccount.org.uk

2. For Lost Pensions: The Pension Tracing Service

It is very common for people to have several small pension pots from different jobs throughout their career. The government's Pension Tracing Service is a free service that can help you find the contact details for a workplace or personal pension scheme.

- **How it works**: The service has a database of over 200,000 pension schemes. It will not tell you whether the person had a pension or how much it is worth, but it will provide you with the contact details for the scheme's administrator, who you can then contact directly.

- **What you need**: You will need the name of the employer or the pension scheme.

- **Website**: gov.uk/find-pension-contact-details

3. For Lost Investments and Shares

Tracing lost investments can be more challenging. There is no central database for shareholdings. However, the three main UK credit reference agencies maintain a register of shareholders in UK companies.

- **How it works**: You can contact Experian, Equifax, or TransUnion to request a search. There may be a small fee for this service.

- **What to look for**: Search through the deceased's paperwork for any old share certificates, dividend statements, or correspondence from company registrars (such as Equiniti, Computershare, or Link Asset Services).

Other Clues to Look For

As an executor, you should play detective and search through the deceased's paperwork for any clues that might lead to a lost asset.

- **Old bank statements**: These can show payments to pension schemes, insurance companies, or investment platforms.

- **Building society passbooks**: Even if a building society has since merged or changed its name, the money is still protected.

- **Payslips**: These will show details of any workplace pension contributions.

- **Tax returns**: These can provide details of investment income or pensions.

***Action Point:** Do not assume that the obvious assets are the only assets. A thorough search for lost accounts and unclaimed assets is a vital part of the executor's role and can make a real difference to the value of the estate.*

The services mentioned in this chapter are free to use. Be cautious of any third-party companies that offer to find lost assets for a large fee or a percentage of the amount found.

Chapter 11: Protecting Your Children: Guardianship and Inheritance

For any parent, the most important consideration when planning for the future is the wellbeing of their children. If the worst were to happen, what would happen to your children? Who would look after them, and how would they be provided for financially? This chapter addresses the critical issues of guardianship and how to ensure your children inherit your assets safely.

Appointing a Guardian: A Parent's Most Important Decision

A guardian is the person you appoint to look after your children if you die before they turn 18. It is a decision that carries immense emotional and practical weight. If you do not formally appoint a guardian, the decision about who will care for your children could be left to the courts, a situation that every parent would want to avoid.

What Happens if No Guardian is Appointed?

- **If one parent dies**: The surviving parent will automatically continue to have parental responsibility.
- **If both parents die**: This is where the situation becomes critical. If no guardian has been appointed in a will, the court will have to appoint someone. This may not be the person you would have chosen, and the uncertainty can be extremely distressing for the children.

How to Appoint a Guardian

The only legally binding way to appoint a guardian is to do so in your will. This is known as a testamentary guardianship appointment.

> **Action Point:** Appointing a guardian is one of the most compelling reasons to make a will. When choosing a guardian, you should discuss your wishes with them first to ensure they are willing and able to take on the role. You should also consider appointing a substitute guardian in case your first choice is unable to act.

Ensuring Your Children Inherit Your Estate

If you leave your estate to your children in your will, they will not be able to inherit it directly until they turn 18. Until then, the inheritance must be held in trust for them. The people who manage this trust are called the trustees. The trustees are usually the same people as the executors of your will.

The Role of Trustees

The trustees are responsible for managing the inheritance on behalf of the children. Their duties include:

- Investing the money prudently to protect and grow its value.

- Making funds available for the children's benefit as they are growing up. This can be for school fees, living expenses, university costs, or other needs.

- Transferring the inheritance to the children once they reach the age specified in the will (usually 18, 21, or 25).

When setting up a trust for your children in your will, you can give your trustees guidance on how you would like the money to be used.

What About Child Trust Funds and Junior ISAs?

Many children have savings in a Child Trust Fund (CTF) or a Junior ISA (JISA). These are tax-free savings accounts for children.

- The death of a parent does not change this. However, the person with parental responsibility for the child will need to become the new registered contact for the account.

- **Accessing the money**: The money in a CTF or JISA is locked away until the child turns 18. At that point, it becomes their money to do with as they wish.

***Important Note:** If a child inherits a large sum of money, it is often sensible to specify in your will that they should not receive it all as a lump sum at 18. You can create a trust that staggers the inheritance, for example, giving them access to a portion at 18, another portion at 21, and the final portion at 25. This can help to protect a young person from being overwhelmed by a large inheritance.*

*Making a will is the only way to be certain that your wishes for your children's care and financial future will be followed. It is the most important document a parent can create.**

Chapter 12: 10 Common Mistakes to Avoid After a Death

Administering an estate is a significant responsibility, and with grief and emotional stress, it is easy to make mistakes. Some errors are minor, but others can have serious legal and financial consequences. This chapter highlights the most common pitfalls and how to avoid them, ensuring a smoother process for you and the beneficiaries.

Mistake 1: Rushing to Pay Bills from Your Own Pocket

When you see bills arriving for the deceased, it can be tempting to pay them immediately from your own money to keep things in order. Do not do this. The deceased's debts must be paid from their estate. You should wait until you have access to the estate's funds after probate. If you pay debts yourself, there is no guarantee you will be able to reimburse yourself, especially if the estate is insolvent (has more debts than assets).

Mistake 2: Distributing the Estate Too Early

Beneficiaries are often anxious to receive their inheritance, but distributing assets before all debts and liabilities have been settled can be a disastrous error. If an unexpected debt emerges after the money has been paid out, the executor can be held personally liable to pay it. Always wait until you have a complete financial picture and have paid all taxes and debts before distributing the estate.

Mistake 3: Missing Time-Sensitive Claims

Several crucial financial benefits have strict deadlines that are easily missed.

- **Bereavement Support Payment**: You must claim within 3 months to get the full amount.

- **ISA Additional Permitted Subscription (APS)**: You have 3 years to use this valuable tax allowance, but it is often forgotten.

- **Deeds of Variation**: If a beneficiary wants to redirect their inheritance, they must do so within 2 years of the death for it to be effective for tax purposes.

Mistake 4: Forgetting to Claim Council Tax Exemption

If the deceased lived alone, their property is exempt from Council Tax until 6 months after probate is granted. If they lived with one other person, that person is now entitled to a 25% Single Person Discount. These benefits are not automatic; you must apply to the local council. Forgetting to do so can cost the estate thousands of pounds.

Mistake 5: Not Searching for Unclaimed Assets

Do not assume you know about all the deceased's assets. Billions of pounds lie in dormant bank accounts, old pensions, and forgotten investments. Use free services like My Lost Account and the Pension Tracing Service to conduct a thorough search. It is your duty as an executor to find all assets.

Mistake 6: Cashing in Premium Bonds Immediately

Premium Bonds remain eligible for the monthly prize draw for 12 months after the holder's death. Any prizes won are paid to the estate, tax-free. There is no harm in leaving them in the draw for this period, and potentially a lot to gain.

Mistake 7: Ignoring the Digital Legacy

In the modern world, a person's digital footprint is a key part of their estate. Social media accounts, email, photo clouds, and online subscriptions all need to be dealt with. Some platforms have legacy settings that can be managed, while others need to be closed down to prevent fraud and identity theft.

Mistake 8: Failing to Secure the Property

If the deceased's property is now empty, it must be secured. This means locking all doors and windows, and importantly, informing the home insurance provider. Many insurance policies have clauses that invalidate the cover if a property is left unoccupied for more than 30 days without notification.

Mistake 9: Misunderstanding Joint Property Ownership

Assuming a property automatically goes into the will is a common error. If a property was owned as 'joint tenants', it automatically passes to the surviving owner and is not part of the estate. If it was owned as 'tenants in common', the deceased's share does form part of the estate and is passed on via their will. You must check the title deeds to be sure.

Mistake 10: Not Keeping Detailed Records

As an executor, you are accountable to the beneficiaries. You must keep meticulous records of every penny in and out of the estate. This includes all assets, debts, administrative costs, and distributions. At the end of the process, you should prepare a final set of estate accounts for the main beneficiaries to approve.

Chapter 13: Critical Deadlines Timeline

When dealing with an estate, timing is everything. Missing a deadline can result in lost benefits, penalties, or unnecessary complications. This chapter provides a comprehensive timeline of the key deadlines you need to be aware of, from the immediate hours after death through to the final distribution of the estate.

Immediate (First 24-48 Hours)

Confirm the Death

If the death occurred at home, you must call a doctor (GP or NHS 111) to confirm the death and issue the Medical Certificate of Cause of Death (MCCD). If the death occurred in hospital or a care home, this will be done automatically.

Inform Close Family

Notify immediate family members and anyone named in the will as an executor or beneficiary.

Arrange Care for Dependents

Ensure that any children, vulnerable adults, or pets are immediately cared for.

Within 5 Days (8 Days in Scotland)

Register the Death

This is a legal requirement. You must register the death at the local Register Office in the district where the person died. You will need the MCCD to do this. The registrar will issue the death certificate and the burial/cremation certificate.

Purchase Multiple Death Certificates

Buy at least 5-10 certified copies of the death certificate. You will need these to send to banks, insurance companies, and other institutions.

Within 3 Months

Claim Bereavement Support Payment (BSP) for Full Amount

If you are eligible for BSP, you must claim within 3 months of your partner's death to receive the full lump-sum payment and all 18 monthly instalments. Claims made after this will result in reduced payments.

Notify the Council for Council Tax Relief

If the deceased lived alone, their property is exempt from Council Tax. If they lived with one other person, that person is now entitled to a Single Person Discount (25% off). Apply to the local council as soon as possible.

Within 6 Months

Pay Inheritance Tax (if due)

If Inheritance Tax is payable, it must be paid by the end of the sixth month after the person's death. Interest will be charged on late payments. Note that you may need to pay at least some of the IHT before you can get the Grant of Probate.

Council Tax Exemption Ends (Post-Probate)

If the deceased's property is empty, it is exempt from Council Tax for up to 6 months after the Grant of Probate is issued. After this, the full charge will apply.

Within 12 Months

Premium Bonds Prize Draw Eligibility Ends

Premium Bonds remain in the monthly prize draw for 12 months after the holder's death. After this, they are automatically cashed in.

Reduced BSP Payments

If you claim BSP between 12 and 21 months after your partner's death, you will not receive the lump-sum payment, but you can still get some monthly instalments.

Within 21 Months

Final Deadline for Bereavement Support Payment

This is the absolute deadline for claiming BSP. After 21 months, you will usually not be able to claim at all (unless the cause of death was only recently confirmed).

Within 2 Years

Deed of Variation Deadline

If a beneficiary wants to redirect their inheritance (for example, to reduce Inheritance Tax), they can execute a Deed of Variation. To be effective for tax purposes, this must be done within 2 years of the date of death.

Within 3 Years

ISA Additional Permitted Subscription (APS) Deadline

The surviving spouse or civil partner has 3 years from the date of death to use their APS allowance. This is a valuable tax benefit that should not be missed.

'In Specie' ISA Transfers

If you are transferring inherited ISA investments 'in specie' (without selling them), you have 180 days from the date the assets are distributed to you to make the transfer.

Ongoing Responsibilities

Keep Beneficiaries Informed

Throughout the administration of the estate, you should keep the main beneficiaries updated on progress. This helps to manage expectations and reduces the risk of disputes.

Prepare Estate Accounts

Before making the final distribution, prepare detailed estate accounts showing all money in and out. Have these approved by the main beneficiaries.

Retain Records

Keep all records and documents for at least 12 years after the estate is fully distributed. This protects you in case of any future queries or disputes.

This timeline is a guide. Always check the specific deadlines that apply to your situation, and seek professional advice if you are unsure.

Who Else to Notify (Beyond Government & Banks)

- **GP/Dentist/Hospitals:** Cancel appointments, return medical equipment

- **Employers:** Payroll, life insurance, pensions

- **Schools/Universities:** Notify pastoral or welfare teams

- **Care providers/social services:** Terminate services and settle invoices

- **Landlord/Mortgage lender:** Secure property arrangements

- **DVLA (vehicle):** Insurer, and leasing/finance companies

- **Pets:** Arrange immediate care; notify microchip database and insurer

Finding Unknown or Lost Pensions

If you don't know the pension provider, use the Pension Tracing Service (GOV.UK).

Phone: 0800 731 0175 (UK) +44 (0)191 218 7777 (abroad)

For free pension guidance, visit MoneyHelper.org.uk or call 0800 011 3797.

Many people have multiple pension pots from different employers throughout their career.

It is common for these to be forgotten, especially if someone changed jobs frequently.

The Pension Tracing Service maintains a database of over 200,000 pension schemes and can help you find the contact details for the scheme administrator.

Support and Wellbeing

It is vital to seek support during this time. Bereavement is one of life's most challenging experiences, and there is no shame in asking for help.

- **Cruse Bereavement Support:** 0808 808 1677 - Freephone national helpline for grief and bereavement support

- **Samaritans:** 116 123 - Free 24/7 helpline for anyone struggling to cope

- **Mind UK:** 0300 123 3393 - Mental health support and information

- **Age UK:** 0800 678 1602 - Support and advice for older people, including bereavement services

Planning Ahead

The best way to help your loved ones after you're gone is to plan ahead. Taking the time now to organise your affairs can save your family enormous stress and uncertainty during an already difficult time.

- Make a Will: This is the single most important document you

  can create

- Store passwords and important documents securely

- Record funeral and memorial wishes

- Keep a list of financial accounts and contacts updated

- Review pension and insurance nominations annually

- Consider a Lasting Power of Attorney

- Share access details with a trusted person

Appendix: Key Contacts

Government Departments

- **HMRC Bereavement Helpline: 0300 322 9620**
  HMRC enquiries relating to a deceased person's tax and
  estate. www.gov.uk/find-hmrc-contacts/bereavement-and-
  deceased-estate-enquiries

- **DWP Bereavement Service: 0800 151 2012**
  Department for Work and Pensions bereavement service
  (e.g., Bereavement Support Payment).
  www.gov.uk/bereavement-support-payment

- **Death Notification Service: 0333 207 6574**
  Notify multiple banks, building societies & financial
  institutions in one call. www.deathnotificationservice.co.uk

- **Pension Tracing Service: 0800 731 0175**
  UK pension tracing (find lost pensions). www.gov.uk/find-
  pension-contact-details

- **NS&I Customer Service: 08085 007 007**
  National Savings & Investments accounts. www.nsandi.com

Major Banks & Insurers (Bereavement Teams)

- Barclays: 0800 068 2238

- HSBC: 0800 085 1992

- Lloyds: 0800 015 0012

- Santander: 0800 587 5870

- NatWest: 0800 161 5903

- Legal & General: 0800 096 6959

- Aviva: 0800 158 3467

- TSB: 0345 835 7834

Appendix: Glossary of Key Terms

Understanding the legal and financial terminology used in estate administration can be challenging. This glossary provides clear definitions of the most important terms you will encounter.

Additional Permitted Subscription (APS)

A special, one-off ISA allowance available to the surviving spouse or civil partner of a deceased ISA holder. It is equal to the value of the deceased's ISA and is in addition to the survivor's normal annual ISA allowance.

Administrator

The person appointed by the court to administer the estate of someone who has died without a valid will (intestate). The administrator has similar duties to an executor.

Beneficiary

A person or organisation who is entitled to receive a share of the deceased's estate, either under the terms of a will or under the rules of intestacy.

Bereavement Support Payment (BSP)

A government benefit paid to the surviving spouse, civil partner, or cohabiting partner of someone who has died. It consists of a lump-sum payment and up to 18 monthly instalments.

Bona Vacantia

Latin for 'vacant goods'. This refers to an estate that passes to the Crown because the deceased died without a will and has no surviving relatives who can inherit under the rules of intestacy.

Continuing Account of a Deceased Investor

An ISA that remains open and retains its tax-free status for a period after the account holder's death. This allows the value of the ISA to continue to grow tax-free while the estate is being administered.

Deed of Variation

A legal document that allows a beneficiary to redirect their inheritance to someone else. If executed within 2 years of death, it can be effective for Inheritance Tax and Capital Gains Tax purposes.

Estate

The total value of all the money, property, and possessions owned by a person at the time of their death, minus any debts and liabilities.

Executor

The person (or people) named in a will to carry out the
deceased's wishes and administer their estate. The executor
has a legal duty to act in the best interests of the beneficiaries.

Grant of Probate

The legal document issued by the Probate Registry that gives
the executor(s) the authority to administer the deceased's
estate. It confirms that the will is valid and that the executor has
the right to act.

Grant of Representation

The general term for the legal authority to administer an estate.
It includes both the Grant of Probate (when there is a will) and
Letters of Administration (when there is no will).

Inheritance Tax (IHT)

A tax on the estate of someone who has died. It is charged at
40% on the value of the estate above the available tax-free
allowances (the Nil-Rate Band and, if applicable, the Residence
Nil-Rate Band).

Intestacy / Intestate

The situation where a person dies without leaving a valid will. Their estate is distributed according to the Rules of Intestacy, a fixed legal framework that determines who inherits.

Joint Tenants

A way of owning property where each owner owns 100% of the property together. When one owner dies, their share automatically passes to the surviving owner(s) by the Right of Survivorship, regardless of what their will says.

Letters of Administration

The legal document issued by the Probate Registry that gives the administrator the authority to deal with the estate of someone who died without a valid will.

Nil-Rate Band (NRB)

The threshold below which no Inheritance Tax is payable. For the 2025/26 tax year, the NRB is £325,000.

Probate

The legal and financial process of administering a deceased person's estate. It involves valuing the estate, paying any taxes and debts, and distributing the remaining assets to the beneficiaries.

Residence Nil-Rate Band (RNRB)

An additional Inheritance Tax allowance available when a person leaves their main home to their direct descendants (children, grandchildren, etc.). For the 2025/26 tax year, the RNRB is £175,000.

Right of Survivorship

The automatic transfer of ownership of an asset (such as a joint bank account or property owned as joint tenants) to the surviving owner(s) when one owner dies.

Rules of Intestacy

The legal framework that determines who inherits the estate of someone who has died without a valid will. The rules follow a strict hierarchy, with spouses, children, and other relatives inheriting in a specific order.

Tenants in Common

A way of owning property where each owner holds a distinct, separate share (for example, 50/50 or 60/40). When one owner dies, their share does not automatically pass to the other owner. Instead, it forms part of their estate and is distributed according to their will or the rules of intestacy.

Testamentary Guardianship

The appointment of a guardian for minor children in a person's will. This is the only legally binding way to ensure that your chosen person will care for your children if you die before they turn 18.

Will

A legal document in which a person sets out their wishes for how their estate should be distributed after their death. It also names the executor(s) who will administer the estate and can appoint guardians for minor children.